# Receiving Comfort from God and Overcoming Grief

Reverend Pamela D. Daniels

# TABLE OF CONTENTS

# INTRODUCTION

I am writing this book from a Christian perspective, and with the help of the Holy Spirit, I am praying that through reading this book you and your loved ones will receive comfort from God and all of the answers you need. I also pray that you will understand that death is not the end for any born-again believer. Instead, it can be a beautiful beginning, especially if your loved one was extremely sick, constantly in pain, unable to accomplish daily tasks, and desperately desiring to go home to be with the Lord.

The Holy Bible in 2 Corinthians 5:8 states, "[Yes] we have confident *and* hopeful courage and are pleased rather to be away from home out of the body and be at home with the Lord." The same verse in the New King James Version (NKJV) reads, "We are confident, yes, well pleased rather to be absent from the body and to be present with the Lord." We can always receive help and comfort from God and the Holy Ghost because the Holy Spirit is our comforter (John 14:26) and "God is a very present *and* well-proved help in trouble" (Psalm 46:1).

We must never allow ourselves to become too afraid, proud, or bitter to ask for God's assistance. In fact, we should always reject bitterness towards God or others because God is never wrong, neither is He ever the problem. He is always the solution to all of our problems, despite what we may feel.

Hebrews 4:16 tells us, "Let us then fearlessly *and* confidently *and* boldly draw near to the throne of grace (the throne of God's unmerited favour to us sinners), that we may receive mercy [for our failures] and find grace to help in good time for every need [appropriate help and well-timed help, coming just when we need it]."

# CHAPTER 1: WILL EVERYONE DIE?

Will everyone die? Sadly, we all will either have to face the enemy death or deal with him in the life of a loved one at some time or the other in our lives. You may be thinking: *Why is Pastor Daniels asking that question? Surely we will all definitely die at one time or the other.* My answer to that is no, everyone will not physically die (Hebrews 11:5 and 2 Kings 2:1-11).

Even though this statement may seem strange to you, please continue reading this book. Don't allow Satan to steal your victory by becoming bitter, angry, and resentful towards God by tearing up this book in anger and tossing it into the garbage bin, because rejection of this message will prevent you from receiving the answers God is longing to give you. Please allow the Holy Spirit to minister to you as you read this book.

Also, we are unwise when we come to a conclusion about any matter before hearing all of the information about it (Proverbs 18:13). We must also be swift to hear, slow to speak, and slow to become angry, because carnal anger does not produce the righteousness God desires. Because the Holy Spirit abides in every born-again believer, all the children of God have the ability to exercise self-control, which is a fruit of the Spirit. Therefore, whenever we are angry, we should refrain from sinning (Galatians 5:22-23; James 1:19-20; Ecclesiastes 7:9; and Ephesians 4:26).

As I support everything that I have to say to you with Scripture from the Holy Bible, God will bear witness with your spirit that I am telling you the truth (Romans 9:1). Holy Scripture also tells us that we should let everything be established in the mouth of two of three witnesses (2 Corinthians 13:1 and Deuteronomy 19:15).

We know that "Jesus Christ (the Messiah) is [always] the same, yesterday, today, [yes] and forever (to the ages)" (Hebrews 13:8). The Holy Bible teaches us that everyone will not die physically. I will give you two biblical examples of people whose physical bodies never died.

## Two Biblical Examples of Believers who Never Saw Death

*Example One*

Enoch continually walked in close fellowship and intimate communion with God for three hundred years after his son Methuselah was born. So pleased was God with Enoch that God translated him into heaven, and he was not seen on earth again. His testimony bore witness of this truth (Genesis 5:21-24 and Hebrews 11:5).

*Example Two*

2 Kings 2 tells the story of Elisha's determination; the prophet went to great lengths in order to receive a double portion of Elijah's spirit. Elijah and Elisha were on their way from Gilgal to Bethel when God was prepared to take Elijah up to heaven by whirlwind (2 Kings 2:1). So Elijah told Elisha to wait in Gilgal, because God had instructed Elijah to go to Bethel. However, Elisha was determined to be with his master Elijah until the end of his earthly life; so he refused to wait there and went with him to Bethel.

Upon his arrival in Bethel, Elisha saw the sons of the prophets approaching. They said to him, "Do you know that the Lord will take your master away from you today?" He said, "Yes, I know it; hold your peace" (2 Kings 2:3). After this confrontation, Elijah instructed Elisha to wait for him there because the Lord had sent him to Jericho. But Elisha refused to be separated from his teacher; so they journeyed to Jericho.

The sons of the prophets who were in Jericho approached Elisha and asked him the same question as the sons of the prophets in Bethel had previously, and his response was the same as before. Elijah commanded his servant Elisha to wait for him in Jericho because God had instructed him to go to the Jordan, but once again Elisha refused to be separated from Elijah. So Elisha accompanied his master to the Jordan together with fifty men, sons of the prophets, who watched Elijah and Elisha from a distance.

Elijah took his mantle, rolled it up, and struck the waters, which divided to the right and the left so that both men crossed over on dry ground. After this miracle, Elisha persevered and stayed with his master until God translated Elijah to heaven and Elisha received a double portion of his spirit (2

Kings 2:9-15). This passage proves that Elijah never died.

## The Rapture of the Church

1 Thessalonians 4:13-18 teaches us that the believers who are alive on the earth will be caught up along with all the resurrected saints in the clouds to meet the Lord, and we shall all be with the Lord forever. This scripture proves that those saints who are alive and experience the rapture will never physically die.

# CHAPTER 2: DEALING WITH GRIEF

## Expressions of Grief

In the days of the Old Testament, people immediately expressed their feelings of grief after someone had died. During this sad period of time, the mourners would rip their clothes, wear sackcloth instead of ordinary clothes, tear out their hair, sprinkle dust and ashes on their heads, and abstain from wearing jewellery. They wept, wailed, and fasted.

Friends would come to the house and visit. Some family members hired professional mourners who wept loudly for hours or days (Matthew 9:23-24; Acts 9:39; and Jeremiah 9:17-18). The family of the deceased also provided food for the mourners.

After the funeral, women usually went to the grave early in the morning to weep and offer prayers.

Mourning usually lasted between seven and thirty days, depending on who had died. After Aaron died, the entire house of Israel wept and mourned for him for thirty days (Numbers 20:29).

However, we must not allow the spirit of grief to attach itself to us and live in a perpetual state of mourning because this is not only unhealthy, but unscriptural also. Even though God sympathized with the children of Israel, though He had great compassion and understood their pains, griefs, sorrows, and purely human reactions, He wanted the Israelites to get on with their lives.

Dearly beloved ones, you, too, can rest assured that your loved ones wouldn't want you to be unhappy, depressed, or suicidal. Neither does God, who is encouraging you to get on with your life. He tells us in scripture that there is a time and a season for everything under the sun (Ecclesiastes 3:1-8).

# Four Biblical Examples of Dealing with Grief

*Example 1*

I will give you four examples about how people dealt with grief, commencing with two examples from David, who was a very successful king. God even calls David a man after His own heart (Acts 13:22).

After the first son of King David and Bathsheba became critically ill, King David petitioned the Lord with much prayer and fasting to heal the child. David lay on the floor all night in grief and prayer. The older servants of his house arose and attempted to lift him off the floor, but he refused to arise and eat with them.

However, despite King David's prayer and fasting, the child died on the seventh day. When the servants heard the sad news, they tried to conceal it from King David, fearing that he would harm himself because he refused to hearken to their counsel while the child was alive. But when King David saw his servants whispering, he immediately perceived that his son had died and asked them if this was true. Unfortunately, they confirmed his worst fears (author's paraphrase 2 Samuel 12:16-19).

Despite this news, "David arose from the ground, washed and anointed himself, and changed his clothes; and he went into the house of the LORD and worshiped. Then he went to his own house; and when he requested, they set food before him, and he ate" (2 Samuel 12:20 NKJV). David showed evidence of his love and commitment towards God by his unselfish act of adoration, genuine praise and worship, even when he was in the midst of such overwhelming grief and pain.

King David's servants were shocked at his unusual response to grief; so they demanded an explanation from him. The king responded by stating that when his son was alive, he had fasted and wept during the dreadful period of illness, desiring that the Lord would be gracious to him and let the child live. Because David's son was already dead and he was incapable of resurrecting him from the dead, David drew comfort from the fact that he would go to him one day and abide in heaven with him, because his son would not return to him.

King David comforted his wife Bathsheba and had sexual intercourse with her, and then she conceived and bore him another son. David called this second son Solomon, and he became a king and the wisest man in the world (2 Samuel 12:20-24 and 1 Kings 4:29-31).

So people deal with grief differently. But we must continue to remain faithful to God no matter how horrible our circumstances are. And after grieving has ceased, resuming a normal life as best as you possibly can is vital.

*Example 2*

After David discovered that King Saul and Jonathan his son had died, David and the men who were with him tore their own clothes. They mourned and wept for King Saul and Jonathan and fasted until evening for the Lord's people and the house of Israel because they were defeated in the battle (2 Samuel 1:11-12).

*Example 3*

Job was a righteous man who lived in the land of Uz. He reverently feared God and abstained from evil. God had abundantly blessed him so that he was the greatest man in the east.

Satan despised this prosperity because he fervently hates God, His people, and everything that concerns Him. So Satan deliberately set out to destroy Job by trying to convince him to curse God and die. Satan tried Job's faith and patience exceedingly. Satan afflicted Job with an abundance of sudden trials, tribulations, and hardships that were nearly too much to bear directly in succession of each other on the same day (Job 1).

The final blow on that day and probably the most painful one occurred when Job received the devastating news from the only surviving messenger informing him of the death of his children. All ten of Job's children had been eating and drinking wine in his eldest son's house, and suddenly a violent gust of wind smote the four corners of the house, causing it to collapse upon his offspring and kill them.

Despite this series of tragic events, God still showed his love and tender mercies by allowing the messenger who delivered the awful news to Job to survive the incident. How much worse it would have been for Job not to know what had happened to his children!

This event reminds me of all of the trouble God went to in order to preserve mankind and the world when He destroyed the world by flood. Though all of the imaginations of man were evil, God preserved Noah, who was righteous, his wife, his three sons, their wives, and some of the males and females of the animal kingdom (Genesis 6-8).

Despite these exceedingly painful, horrific, sudden tragedies, Job continued to excel in the fruit of the Spirit. Job exercised great strength, patience, stamina, faithfulness, godly character, integrity, commitment, and loyalty towards God by arising in his grief-stricken state, tearing his robe, shaving his head, and genuinely worshipping God in the beauty of holiness and in spirit and in truth. What a wonderful example Job set to mankind (Job 1:20-22; Galatians 5:22-23; John 4:4; and Psalm 96:9)!

Unlike many of us, Job didn't turn to anything or anyone to numb the pain he felt. He could have turned to food or abused drugs, alcohol, or any other substance, but he blessed and magnified God's name in worship. He boasted in the Lord and made God exceedingly bigger and greater than all of his problems. He refused to focus on his problems, complain, sin, or accuse God foolishly, even though in the world's eyes he had good reason to do so. Instead, Job submitted completely to God in worship and resisted the devil (James 4:7).

When we follow Job's wonderful example by worshipping God despite our many tears, sorrows, and hardships and magnify Him in praise, we will receive comfort from God and experience supernatural peace, joy, strength, and His awesome presence in ways we've never imagined were possible. We will find that "the joy of the Lord is our strength," that "God inhabits the praises of His people," and that "in His presence there's the fullness of joy and at His right hand there are pleasures forevermore" (Psalm 22:3, 16:11; and Nehemiah 8:10).

Also, because God enjoys the prosperity of His servants and He is the Great Restorer, He will give you beauty for ashes, joy for mourning, and probably double for your trouble like He did for Job, because He is no respecter of persons (Psalm 35:27; Isaiah 61:3; Joel 2:25; and Job 42:10, 12). "Weeping may endure for a night, But joy *comes* in the morning" (Psalms 30:5 NKJV). And one day with the Lord is equivalent to a thousand years (2 Peter 3:8). So be patient. Recovery takes time.

*Example 4*

Here's an example of how Joshua and the Israelites dealt with grief after Moses the servant of the Lord had died. They mourned Moses' death in the plains of Moab for thirty days, and then weeping and mourning ceased (Deuteronomy 34:7-8).

Then the Lord commanded Joshua to arise, take his place, go over to Jordan together with the people into the land that He had promised to give the Israelites (Joshua 1:1-2). God our heavenly father is an extremely loving Father who desires the best for all of His children.

He does not want anyone to remain in a perpetual state of mourning, which is not normal or good for us; neither would our deceased ones require this permanent sadness of us. Our beloved ones would definitely want us to be happy and to resume a normal life as soon as we possibly could. Some of them, especially the born-again believers, would want us to rejoice that they are in a better place, completely free from all pain, suffering, and sorrow (Revelation 21:4).

So do yourself a big favour and cheer up. If you don't want to seek joy for yourself, do so for the others who are left behind. Besides, this prolonged sadness and depression can be detrimental to your health, while laughter is good for your health, like medicine (Proverbs 17:22). Therefore, refuse guilt and condemnation from the devil as you return to a normal life (Romans 8:1; John 8:44, 10:10; and Revelation 12:10).

# CHAPTER 3: OVERCOMING GRIEF

## Forgive Others and Receive Comfort

Don't ever hesitate to ask God to comfort and strengthen you, as His hands are not too short to reach down and pull you out of any pit you may find yourself in (Isaiah 59:1). As the healing process begins and you become stronger you should also ask God to show you if you have any areas of un-forgiveness or bitterness towards Him, anyone or anything. If He reveals any area of un-forgiveness in your life immediately ask Him to help you forgive quickly as un-forgiveness will hinder your recovery from the grieving process. When we reflect on how much God loves and has forgiven us, forgiving others will become much easier (Romans 8:31-39; John 3:16; Romans 5:8;

Matthew 6:9-15, 18:21-22; Luke 23:34; 1 John 1:9; and Isaiah 43:25).

## Trust God to Bring You Out

The Holy Bible commands everyone in Proverbs 3:5-6 (NKJV) to "trust in the LORD with all *your* heart, And lean not on *your* own understanding; In all *your* ways acknowledge Him, And He shall direct *your* paths" (italics mine).

In addition to this command, we must remember that the Holy Spirit is our Comforter and Helper. Knowing that Jesus is the original Comforter, we can find comfort in Him also. Therefore, ask the Holy Spirit to comfort you, and take the time to receive that much-needed comfort from Him (John14:16-18).

We can also draw comfort from the fact that God is always with us despite how lonely or isolated we may feel. God is definitely a present help in a time of trouble; so trust God. Depend, lean heavily upon Him, because He is extremely faithful, reliable, and trustworthy. Ask Him to bring you out of this difficult, dark time, and I can assure you from experience that He will somehow bring you out, despite how impossible any help might seem to you in the natural realm (1 Corinthians 10:13; Psalm 121:1-2, 46:1, 16:11; Hebrews 13:5-6; and Matthew

19:26). Even though this statement may be extremely hard to believe, God may eventually bring something good out of your present situation (Genesis 50:20 and Job 42:10-17).

## Remember that You Are Not Alone

Remember that you are the only one going through tough times (Ecclesiastes 1:9 and John 16:33). Besides the fact that God has his remnant everywhere, He has also faithfully promised to never leave us nor forsake us (Hebrews 13:5). Therefore, you are never alone, despite how you feel.

Don't allow yourself to be deceived into thinking that you are the only child of God going through trials, like Elijah did when he thought that he was the only prophet of the Lord who remained after Jezebel had cut off the prophets of Lord (1 Kings 18:22). Even though the enemy appeared to be strong and Baal had 450 prophets in Israel, God was stronger than Baal.

Elijah slew the 450 prophets of Baal (1 Kings 18:40). Shortly afterward, Elijah received a threatening message from Jezebel by messenger stating that within a day, she would ensure that

Elijah would be dead like the prophets whom he had killed.

Elijah immediately became afraid and fled for his life out of Jezebel's realm. He fell asleep under a juniper tree. An angel appeared before him, touched him, and told him to arise and eat. When Elijah awoke and looked around, he saw a cake baked on coals and a bottle of water. Elijah ate and drank and resumed sleeping.

When the angel of the Lord next appeared, he touched Elijah again and commanded him to eat, saying that the journey was too great for him. So Elijah did as he was commanded and went in the strength of the food which he had just consumed for forty days and forty nights to Horeb, the mountain of God. What an awesome miracle God had performed! When Elijah arrived there, he saw a cave there where he could live.

God asked Elijah what he was doing there. He responded by saying, "I have been very zealous for the Lord God of hosts; because the children of Israel have forsaken Your covenant, torn down Your altars, and killed Your prophets with the sword. I alone am left; and they seek to take my life" (1 Kings 19:14 NKJV).

However, Elijah did not speak the truth completely because, even though Jezebel threatened Elijah's life, Obadiah had hidden 100 of the Lord's prophets in fifties in a cave and fed them with bread and water (1 Kings 18:3-4), and Obadiah had told Elijah what he had done. Therefore, Elijah knew that at least 101 of God's prophets were alive, including himself. And after Elijah responded to God, God gave him some duties to perform, and the Lord informed Elijah that 7000 prophets in Israel had abstained from worshipping Baal.

Therefore, be wise to the wiles of the devil, and refuse to listen to him or believe his lies when he tells you that you are the only one going through tribulations. Ecclesiastes 1:9 also tells us that there is nothing new under the sun. Immediately remember that Satan is the father of all liars and everything that is false. Therefore he is incapable of telling the truth (John 8:44).

## Tell God how You Are Feeling

Some of you may be thinking: *Why should I tell God how I'm feeling? He already knows everything* (Hebrews 4:13). And you may be ignorantly and angrily thinking that He is the source of all your problems because, although you fervently prayed, pleaded, and beseeched Him to heal your loved one, He never answered your prayer. How could God be so hard-hearted, rude, callous and unkind? You know that God (Love) is never rude or unkind (1 Corinthians 13:4-5), but you don't understand why God could have allowed this tragedy to befall you. After all, you're a good person, and so was your sweet, deceased, beloved one.

Dearly beloved, you are not thinking clearly. Yes, God is all-knowing, but "we know in part and we prophesy in part. And we see in a mirror, dimly," (1 Corinthians 13:9, 12 NKJV). So we must not become high-minded and exalt our thoughts above His, because His ways and thoughts are higher than ours; besides, the creation is never greater than the Creator (Isaiah 55:8-9; Psalm 47:2).

Therefore, I strongly admonish you to repent immediately for thinking such ugly thoughts about God, let alone expressing them through speech. We should never judge anyone, especially not God, who is the judge of all (Luke 6:37 and James 4:11-12). Yes, God is love, and He is certainly never unkind or rude. When you fail to receive the answers you desire, God is not ignoring you. God knows best, and He is never wrong.

Despite all of this instruction, I understand how you feel. And dealing with grief biblically can be difficult and rather frustrating when you have done all that you know to do: standing on the Word of God, keeping positive confessions, never saying the wrong thing, (and immediately repenting if it happens by accident), and caring for your loved one by providing the correct foods, helping with exercise, and following the doctor's instructions exactly. When your beloved one dies, your disappointment and grief can turn to anger and blame.

## Know that God Is Always Good

However, you must remember that God is always good. So stop blaming Him for all of the bad things that happen in your life. He has only good plans for your life, and He delights greatly in the prosperity of His servants (Jeremiah 29:11 and Psalm 35:27). He is completely innocent of all wrongdoing and has absolutely nothing to do with evil or sin (2 Corinthians 5:21).

Therefore, we must never allow any root of bitterness to enter into our souls. Neither should we ever make the same mistake as John the Baptist did. John the Baptist became offended at Jesus after he lovingly corrected King Herod of his wicked sin by telling him it was unlawful for him to have Herodias, his brother's Philip's wife.

However, instead of humbling himself and repenting of his sin, King Herod became enraged and offended at John, continued to err, and wrongfully arrested and imprisoned John the Baptist, who was completely innocent of any wrongdoing.

John the Baptist was imprisoned for serving God and doing right. So John's offence towards Jesus became a stumbling block in his life, causing him to be beheaded and die prematurely without completely fulfilling his God-given assignment.

However, the Holy Bible teaches us that we are pleasing and acceptable to God when we are punished for doing right and taking it patiently (1 Peter 2:20). When we do so, God will vindicate, reward, and protect us as He did Daniel, Shadrach, Meshach, and Abednego (Daniel 3, 6). James 1:12

(NKJV) confirms this reward by stating, "Blessed *is* the man who endures temptation; for when he has been approved, he will receive the crown of life which the Lord has promised to those who love Him."

There will always be times of testing in our lives when we are treated unfairly, even when we are doing the right thing, and during those times, we can easily become mad and offended at God. But mature Christians will endure hardship like good soldiers, refusing to be offended at God or man and allowing the trials to produce godly character. When we respond to them rightly, these trials can bring us closer to God instead of driving us away from Him, and our closeness to God can cause Satan great distress in the process by defeating him at his own game (Matthew 11:6; 2 Timothy 2:3; and James 4:8).

Despite what you are suffering, don't reciprocate evil with evil and be overcome with evil, but keep on doing the right thing. Remember that all who live godly lives will suffer persecution (Romans 12:17, 21; and 2 Timothy 3:12). Job overcame evil with good when he prayed for his friends, even though they doubted his integrity, and God rewarded him by giving him double for his trouble (Job 42:10).

I absolutely refuse to become offended at God, and so should you, dearly beloved, because God is not the culprit behind our problems. Satan is. God does not rob, steal, kill, or destroy. He is the author of life, of all that is good and perfect, and He is the author and finisher of our faith (see John 10:10; James 1:17; 1 Timothy 6:17; 2 Peter 1:3; Hebrews 12:2; and Genesis 1, 2, paying particular attention to verses 1:26-28, and 2:7).

As I'm in the process of completing this book, I am faithfully serving God, seeking Him, and walking in His will for my life. And I'm trying to bring comfort to you and many others who are reading this book. Right now, I, too, have been attacked by the exceedingly wicked devil. I have been given the opportunity, exactly like you, to become offended and mad with God (the only one who can truly help us). A few days ago, a close relative of mine was robbed and brutally shot at his place of employment for no apparent reason apart from a few bucks and some food. My relative died shortly after his arrival at the hospital.

This death was completely unprovoked, unwarranted, tragic, sudden, and absolutely senseless. This very kind and loving young man has left a mother who has already suffered the terrible loss of burying a younger son. That younger son died prematurely several years ago, and the mother is probably still trying somehow to come to terms with his loss. Now, in addition to that horrible tragedy, she is also grieving over her second son's brutal murder. God's perfect will is that no parents should have to bury their own children. This perversion goes against nature. Children should always outlive their parents.

Sadly, the mother of these two lost boys may be wondering: *Oh Lord, how much more can I take? Where were you when I needed you most?* What I can tell this dear one and you, too, is that God was right there with you, and He still is (Hebrews 13:5). He can certainly relate to your pain, because He is the Great High Priest who can be touched with our feelings of infirmities (Hebrews 4:14-16). And even though you may feel alone in your grief now, you're definitely not the only person who has asked God these questions.

I will give you another example of someone who can relate to your pain. The son of a born-again Christian pastor and believer who really loved God was tragically electrocuted and died in church when he was faithfully serving God helping in the lighting department. Devastated, this pastor asked God:

*Where were You when my son died?* The Lord responded by saying: *Exactly in the same place where I was when my Son was being crucified.*

Yes, even though Jesus is the expressed image of God and His completely sinless, perfect, and holy only begotten Son, soldiers mocked, humiliated, whipped, and brutally crucified Him on the cross at Calvary (John 3:16-18; Luke 23).

Even though you're broken-hearted and you don't understand why your beloved one was snatched away prematurely from you, trust God, and He will bring you out of this dark, despondent place, even though you may not be able to comprehend how (1 Corinthians 10:13 and Isaiah 59:1). God will also give you the comfort and peace you need (John 14:27).

Now, returning to the brutal, senseless murder of my dearly beloved, deceased relative. Sadly, he also left a young, grieving widow, two children, a brother, a father, and many other relatives behind.

So, dearly beloved, I can relate with your loss, pain, and grief because, in addition to my recent loss, I, too, have suffered the loss of many cherished, loved friends and family members who I held dearly in my heart. And some of these people appeared to have been some of the sweetest and kindest people that I have ever had the pleasure of meeting. Even though I and my hurting family members are going through a very painful and dark time, I draw comfort from the precious, wonderful times that I and these deceased ones had together, knowing that they wouldn't want me to mourn their loss eternally, but to somehow continue with my life.

This knowledge also helps me to be thankful for the other people God has placed in my life and to love and cherish them even more, making the most out of our time together and refusing to fuss and fight with them over silly things that can be quickly and easily resolved (Ephesians 5:15-16).

Therefore, I strongly advise everyone reading this book to immediately forgive everyone who has ever hurt them. Make things right before sending your children to school, leaving your home, going to sleep, et cetera. Don't ever leave home mad at your spouse, children, or loved ones, but resolve things quickly before you go. Tell them how much you love, cherish, and appreciate them.

I know that some people are more difficult to love than others are. If for some reason you're struggling to love someone, ask God to help you to do so with the love of God that has been shed abroad in your heart by the Holy Ghost. Never take anyone for granted, because you never know when may be the last time you will ever see anyone (Romans 5:5; and Ephesians 4: 26-27).

## Get Busy Helping Someone Else

I have experienced suffering as a pastor. In addition to grieving over my lost ones, many times I have had to counsel others through what appeared to be minute issues in comparison to what was happening in my own life. However, God has always helped me put aside my pain and my own needs to assist those hurting people.

I can remember when I was going through a tough time financially in my local church assembly as a full-time minister. The pain was so overwhelming when I was standing at the book table by the door trying to sell my Christian books and teaching materials, sadly to no avail. I almost burst into tears when many people just kept passing by and everyone seemed completely oblivious to my pain.

However, I greeted a lady as she was passing by, enquiring how she was, and she broke down and vehemently wept in my arms. Somehow with God's help, I controlled my emotions, prayed for her, and warmly embraced, comforted, and ministered the love of God to her. In so doing, I was able to get my eyes off my own problems and bear someone else's burdens, fulfilling the law of Christ (Galatians 6:2).

So I can promise you from experience that caring for another person not only helps the person you help to recover, but it also helps to ease your pain. When you take your eyes off your problems and keep yourself busy helping others, you will find that it's truly more blessed to give and help others than to receive. When we do so, we experience a two-fold blessing (Acts 20:35).

To obtain healing and overcome depression and self-centeredness, refuse to indulge in self-pity continually, and get busy helping others overcome their problems. These acts of kindness help you to recover in addition to letting your light shine and bear the fruit of the Spirit, such as love, joy, kindness, and peace. Ministering to others helps you to feel better about yourself, and in the process of ministry, you will become more like Jesus (Matthew 5:16; Galatians 5:22-23; and Ephesians 5:1).

Jesus, who is completely selfless, shows us the perfect example of how to walk in love, even when we are grieving and mourning. Matthew 14 gives an accurate account of John the Baptist's barbaric and brutal murder. John was Jesus' first cousin, the same one who was filled with the Holy Ghost in the womb of his mother Elizabeth and who came to make the way for Jesus (Luke 1:15).

Jesus only learned of John's sudden, tragic, and unprovoked murder after his burial. Stricken with grief, a deep sense of loss, anguish, and almost unbearable pain, He withdrew Himself privately into a boat and travelled to a solitary place. Under these horrific circumstances, I believe He definitely needed to get away from everyone and everything else and spend time alone with His loving Father God to be comforted and to overcome His sudden and overwhelming grief.

However, a large multitude of people followed Him by land on foot from the towns. Under the circumstances, Jesus had every right to be angry and to send the large multitudes of people away empty-handed while He received much-needed comfort and counsel from His loving Father. But He refused to do so. He set aside **all** of His current needs and had compassion, deep pity, and sympathy for everyone, even curing the sick. He excelled in extreme agape love, patience, and kindness.

In addition, when the evening came He refused to take the foolish counsel from His disciples and send the large multitudes of people away fasting. Jesus loved the multitudes. He didn't want anyone to collapse on the way to the villages to purchase food; so He commanded His disciples to give them something to eat. But His disciples refused to do so, saying: "We have here only five loaves and two fish" (Matthew 14:17 NKJV).

Even though He was emotionally drained and exhausted, Jesus commanded His disciples to bring the food to Him, and He commanded the crowds to sit down on the grass. Instead of complaining like most people would have done under these circumstances, He took the five loaves and two fishes and honoured His Father by looking up to heaven and thanking Him for the provision. He blessed and broke the loaves, gave them to the disciples, and the disciples gave bread to the people.

When everyone had finished eating and was completely satisfied, the disciples picked up the remaining broken fragments and placed them into twelve baskets, which were completely full. Five thousand men had eaten, excluding the women and children. What an exciting and miraculous day this must have been for the people!

However, as if this miracle wasn't already enough, at the end of an extremely tiring, long, hard, day, Jesus proceeded to direct His disciples to go into the boat and cross over to the other side before Him while He sent the multitudes away. Then He went up alone into the mountains to pray and stayed there until the evening.

But the disciples encountered a horrific storm on their way over to the other side of the lake as the contrary wind and waves battered their boat. On the fourth watch of the night, Jesus approached them, walking on the sea. They immediately became terrified when they saw Him, screaming: "It is a ghost!" (Matthew 14:26 NKJV).

Jesus instantly and lovingly reached out to them, telling them to be courageous and not to be afraid, assuring them that it was Him. Then Peter responded, saying "'Lord, if it is You, command me to come to You on the water.' So He said, 'Come.' And when Peter had come down out of the boat, he walked on the water to go to Jesus" (Matthew 14:28-29 NKJV).

However, because of the boisterous wind, Peter became afraid, began to sink, and cried out to the Lord for His assistance. Jesus immediately reached out, saved him, rebuked him because of his little faith, and demanded an explanation as to why he doubted. Then Peter accompanied Jesus into the boat, and the wind ceased (Matthew 14:30-32).

The other disciples in the boat began to worship Jesus, saying, "Truly You are the Son of God" (Matthew 14:33 NKJV). They crossed over safely and arrived at Gennesaret. When the men from Gennesaret recognized Jesus, they brought everyone in the surrounding regions who was sick to Him, and they beseeched Him to touch the fringe of His garment. Everyone who touched it was perfectly restored (authors' paraphrase Matthew 14:35-36).

As imitators of God, we, too, can go out of our way to express love and help others even when we're hurting and in need of help ourselves. When we do so, we sow a good deed seed which will return to us in a good measure when we need it most (Luke 6:36, 38 and Galatians 6:7).

Remember that God is **not** the source of your problems; Satan is. He is the thief who only comes to steal, kill, and destroy. But God is the only one who can really help us either by directly intervening or by allowing other people to do so. He is the source of every good and perfect gift and the author of abundant life, not the author of death (Psalm 121:1-2; Hebrews 12:2; Genesis 1; James 1:17; and John 10:10).

We must refuse to become puffed up and prideful. We must be humble and lowly, esteeming others higher than we do ourselves, not having an exaggerated opinion by being deceived into thinking that we are much wiser than we really are. God is exceedingly wiser than all of us put together, neither do we know everything. For we know in part, prophesy in part, and see things darkly through a glass (1 Corinthians 13:9, 12).

# CHAPTER 4: YOU ARE NOT ALONE

Dearly beloved, while you are suffering, don't allow the devil to sow seeds of doubt into your heart and deceive you into thinking that God does not love you anymore and that you have to go through this trial all by yourself. In fact, this doubt is far from the truth, because the Holy Spirit (the Comforter) abides in believers forever; nothing can ever separate us from God's love (John 3:16, 14:15-18 and Romans 8:35-39). To illustrate that you are not alone, I will give three examples of people who died of sickness or disease and did not receive their healings, even though their loved ones prayed and asked God to heal them.

# Three People who Died Despite Prayer

*Example 1*

One young man for some reason or the other believed that he would die before he reached age forty, and he constantly told people that he would die by age forty. Shortly before his fortieth birthday, he became critically ill and went into a coma.

Brother Hagin was summoned to the hospital to pray for his recovery. As the prophet began to pray, God forbade his prayers, because the young man had spoken stout words against himself. Unfortunately, those words could not be reversed because he was already in a coma.

The words we speak about ourselves are of paramount importance. We have the ability to speak either life or death with our own tongues, though God wisely commands us to choose life (Proverbs 18:21 and Deuteronomy 30:19). Therefore, we should only say things that we desire to come to pass in our lives.

I believe that if the deceased had gone into a coma when he was a young child, his parents would have been able to override the stout words he had carelessly spoken over his own life. He could have fully recovered and lived, because they had spiritual authority over him.

However, the young man sadly believed in his heart that he would die, confessed it with his mouth, and his words became his reality. So choose your words wisely before speaking, only saying what you really desire.

*Example 2*

Another man became terminally ill, and he and his wife prayed and asked God to heal him. They were both born-again Christians, and to the best of his wife's knowledge, the two of them did everything they knew to get him well.

They believed, confessed, and stood on the Word of God. In addition, they followed the doctors' instructions, completely obeying and doing everything he instructed them to do, including changing his diet. After striving so hard physically and spiritually, the man would usually recover for a time, but his health was always a constant battle.

Unknown to his wife, the man became tired of fighting his constant battle with illness, gave up in his mind, quit fighting, and desired to go home to be with the Lord. So when he died, his wife was shocked, because she incorrectly thought that they both stood in faith for his healing and believed that he would recover completely.

However, instead of blaming God, she and another godly person wisely prayed and asked God why her husband had died and not recovered from the illness. Afterwards, someone discovered her deceased husband's diary and read it. Its contents revealed his mental exhaustion and desire to be with the Lord. He also stated that even though he'd confessed with his mouth that he believed he was healed to his wife, he didn't really believe in his healing or even desire to recover. Proverbs 23:7 tells us that as a man thinks in his heart, so is he. For this man, the thoughts of his heart led to his death.

After discovering this diary, the wife was no longer confused. She had peace with God and accepted the situation. God has given us choice and willpower, and He will never override our willpower; neither can we override anyone else's will. That respect is the reason why everyone definitely won't be saved, even though God desires the salvation of the world (Deuteronomy 30:19; 1 Timothy 2:4; and Matthew 7:13-14).

*Example 3*

The final example is a story about a married couple who were very successful in the corporate business world. The wife was a Holy Spirit-filled, born-again believer, but the husband was not.

After years of faithfulness to God, prayer for her husband's salvation, and standing on the Word of God, this wife saw her husband finally give his life to the Lord and became a born-again Christian. Both the man and his wife were strong Christians. On fire for the Lord, they went into Christian ministry.

However, the husband suddenly became terminally ill with cancer. The couple stood on the Word of God, confessed, meditated on healing scriptures, prayed the prayer of faith, and had many well-known ministers with proven healing ministries praying for him.

This man changed his diet, consuming lots of fruits and vegetables, et cetera. He also fully followed the instructions of his physician. The couple did all they knew to do in the natural realm and the spiritual realm for this man to receive his healing. He appeared to be getting better, but suddenly he had a relapse and died.

His wife became confused; so she and another person who had spiritual authority in her life prayed and sought the Lord for answers as to why this death occurred.

The Lord reminded them that her husband was a very successful business man before he became a Christian. And even though he had planned to seek the Lord with all of his heart and do the same in ministry, the pull of the world would have been too much for him. If the man had received his healing, he would have returned to a sinful lifestyle and backslidden.

Because nothing is hidden from God and because He is tender hearted, loving, kind, merciful, and always mindful of our best interests, the Lord took this man home to be with Him in order to deliver his soul from eternal damnation in hell (Mark 9:43-48).

When the widow woman received this answer from God along with the confirmation from her friend who stood in faith with her, her understanding cleared up all of the confusion in her mind. She received comfort from God and was able to put the situation to rest.

Even though we don't understand everything God does, He knows the end from the beginning. So we must trust God in every circumstance, giving Him thanks in everything and for everything, despite how we feel (Ephesians 5:20 and 1 Thessalonians 5:18).

If Jesus had gone by His feelings, He never would have submitted completely to the will of His Father and died the painful and humiliating death on the cross at Calvary. But He endured the cross, despising the shame, so that everyone could be saved (Hebrews 12:2).

In addition to reading this book, I strongly recommend that you read my book **God Is Willing to Make You Whole** which has an entire chapter entitled *Why Do People Fail to Receive Their Healings?* This teaching will be of great help to you if you are still confused, wondering why your loved ones have passed away.

## Our Great High Priest Understands How We Feel

Telling God how you feel will help you to recover more quickly. We should speak to God openly and honestly, bringing everything into the open. Bottling up emotions in our heart and holding malice towards God and others does us no good. In fact, this kind of withholding opens the door for the devil, allowing him to build strongholds in our minds. Besides, no matter how hard you try, you cannot hide anything from God, because He knows everything.

Jesus lovingly commands everyone who is heavy laden and burdened to come to Him, for He has promised to give us rest. He also instructs us to cast our cares upon Him because He cares for us. Casting our cares includes telling Him about all of our problems and depending on Him to **fix** them (Matthew 11:28-30; Psalm 55:22; and 1 Peter 5:7).

Even though we are not talking about our own personal sins here, we can look to King David, who received forgiveness for the sins he had committed with Bathsheba. The prophet Nathan confronted David, who confessed his sins to Nathan and God. David was forgiven, and he experienced a more intimate relationship with God (2 Samuel 12:13 and Psalm 51).

God understands us, relates to us, and sympathises with us. He is our Great High Priest who can be touched with our feelings of infirmities (Hebrews 4:15). Imagine how God felt when His only begotten, completely innocent, sinless, perfect, righteous, and holy Son died on the cross to redeem sinful men (Luke 23; and Ephesians 1:7).

Out of unconditional, eternal, agape love, God gave us everything that He had. Jesus was the perfect sacrifice for sin. Because of His death, priests would no longer have to sacrifice animals to atone for sin for a year, repeating the same sacrifices yearly (Hebrews 10:1-20).

Jesus was a man of sorrows and acquainted with grief. He was rejected when He came to His own and they knew Him not (Isaiah 53:3-4; and John 1:11). However, Jesus was the first born of many sons. So if anyone can understand what you're suffering, Jesus definitely can. He feels your pain, and He's longing to deliver you.

## Receive Counselling and Help from Others

Don't buy into the lies of the devil that a problem shared is a problem doubled. The great apostle Paul instructs us in Galatians 6:2 to bear each other's burdens. When we do so, we are walking in love. Neither should you be too prideful to receive counsel from others. God may use Christians and sometimes non-Christians to advise you and help you on your way. So don't dismiss any counsel that aligns with scripture simply because the person who offered it is not born-again.

I will give you an example of how God used an unbeliever to prophesy over my life. One day I was leaving to attend a baptism service at church. A friend of mine said to me, "You're going to attend a baptism; you'll be the next one to be baptized." Sure enough, a few months later I was baptized.

Seeing that both Christians and non-Christians have experienced the loss of loved ones, under God's direction both can offer you great advice, comfort, and help. God can use any vessel He chooses. Remember, He used a donkey to speak to Balaam (Numbers 22:29-30).

## Don't Hold Your Feelings Inside

Share your feelings, especially with others who have experienced the loss of loved ones. These people may be able to tell you how they dealt with the situation. Even though you may feel that you will never be able to recover from this dark and stressful time in your life, you maybe able to see a little light at the end of the tunnel. God is no respecter of persons. He will bring you out of emotional darkness, exactly as He brought them out of it (Acts 10:34). You may be able to draw strength, comfort, and wisdom from what fellow sufferers have to say. And listening to them will also help you to realize that you are not alone.

I can remember when my only and very beloved aunt passed away. The grief was not easy for me and the rest of the family to bear. My mother and eldest brother went to America to offer support and comfort the family who lived there. But I remained in England along with several other family members.

Before my aunt died, I had pre-arranged to launch my public Christian Ministry and host a gospel meeting on the same day of her funeral, in addition to hosting a series of meetings pre-booked in the future. Because I had prayed ahead of time and had peace in my heart to move forward, I knew that this grief was Satan attacking me directly to prevent me from launching my Christian Ministry and doing the work of the Lord. I knew that I had to proceed with the ministry and stay in England to support other family members here also.

So I persevered and hosted the Gospel meeting. That night, three people were born again in our first public meeting. If I had attended the funeral service in America or cancelled the service because of my grief, I would never have made the altar call and seen those three precious people born again in the church service that evening.

I thank and praise God for coming through for me in such a miraculous way and allowing me to lead those special people to the Lord. So God can make something good happen, even in the midst of the most painful, sad, horrific, and tragic circumstances. I pray in Jesus' name that this testimony will encourage you during the period of your recovery.

## Don't Isolate Yourself from Others

Don't isolate yourself and neglect your loved ones and other family members. And certainly don't take your anger out on your spouse, children, loved ones, and others whom God has placed in your life to help you. Don't mistreat them or reject them because you are hurting.

Remember that they love you and have your best interests at heart. They are grieving and are hurting exactly like you are, or even more so. So in their time of affliction, they certainly don't need your rejection. They definitely need your love, comfort, support, and understanding.

Refuse to be selfish. Resist the spirit of strife, and draw strength and comfort from each other. Use for good what Satan meant for your harm. Draw closer to God, your family members, and your loved ones (James 4:8). And confidently trust God to bring something good somehow out of this awful situation, just as He did for Joseph.

Joseph's brothers sold him to some Ishmaelites, who took him down to Egypt and sold him to Potiphar, an officer of Pharaoh. Despite all of this pain and unjust suffering, the Lord was with Joseph, causing everything he did to prosper and succeed. Even though Joseph was a slave, he became a prosperous and successful man (Genesis 39:1-3).

Joseph pleased Potiphar exceedingly, causing Potiphar to favour and promote Joseph. His master put Joseph in charge of everything he had. Because of Joseph's care, Potiphar had to take no care for anything apart from the food that he ate.

Possibly due to Potiphar's carelessness and his lack of interest and attention, as well as Joseph's extreme attractiveness, Potiphar's wife became consumed with a burning lust and desire for Joseph. So she tried to seduce him, but Joseph maintained his integrity and remained faithful to God. She was unsuccessful despite her many attempts.

However, one day Joseph went into the house to perform his duties. While all of the other men of the house were outside the premises, Potiphar's wife grabbed Joseph by his garment and tried to persuade him to have sexual intercourse with her. But Joseph refused and immediately ran away, leaving his garment in her hand.

When this woman discovered that she had his garment in her hand, she called to the men of the house, who then returned to the premises. She told them that her husband Potiphar had brought in a Hebrew to mock and insult them. She then began making false allegations, saying that Joseph had attempted to rape her and that he fled and left his garment in her hand when she screamed out loudly.

She kept Joseph's garment with her and repeated the same lies to her husband when he returned home. Upon hearing his wife's disgusting accusations, Potiphar became enraged and immediately put Joseph in prison. This punishment was completely unwarranted, because Joseph was not even given a fair trial.

But God was with Joseph, showering him with an abundance of loving kindness and tender mercies. God gave Joseph favour with the prison warden, who committed every prisoner in the prison into Joseph's loving care. Joseph prospered because God was with him. God made everything Joseph did to prosper and succeed (Genesis 37, 39; Hebrews 13:5; and Psalm1:1-3, 121:1-2).

One day, two of the prisoners' countenances were unusually sad. Joseph became concerned because he genuinely cared about all of the prisoners' well-being; so he enquired why. Both of the sad men were former employees of Pharaoh. One was a butler, and the other was a baker. They both had distressing dreams that troubled them deeply. They told Joseph their dreams, and with God's help, Joseph interpreted them correctly.

But sadly, the interpretation of the baker's dream was undesirable. Joseph told him that within three days of his dream, he would be beheaded, hung on a tree, and left unburied. Birds would consume his flesh. Unfortunately for the baker, this prophecy came true.

However, in contrast to the baker's bleak prophecy, the butler's dream had an extremely happy outcome. Joseph told him that within three days Pharaoh would restore him to his former position, and he would once again serve Pharaoh as his butler. This interpretation, of course, made the butler extremely happy.

However, Joseph asked the butler to remember him and show him kindness when he was restored to his former position. Joseph asked the butler to tell Pharaoh about his accurate interpretations of dreams. Joseph also asked the butler to explain that Joseph was completely innocent of any wrongdoing and was unlawfully imprisoned.

But sadly, the butler completely forgot about Joseph when he was restored to his former position, neither did he deliver Joseph's message to Pharaoh. Despite this misfortune, Joseph didn't complain. Instead of becoming bitter, he continued to serve faithfully with excellence in the prison, doing his job wholeheartedly as unto the Lord (Colossians 3:22-24).

Two years later, Pharaoh had two dreams which greatly distressed him. So he desperately sought the interpretation of them from all of the magicians and wise men of Egypt, but sadly to no avail.

When Pharaoh's butler heard of this dilemma, he finally remembered how Joseph had accurately interpreted his dream along with the baker's and told Pharaoh about him. So Pharaoh sent for Joseph, who was hastily brought out of the dungeon and told Pharaoh's dreams. With God's help, Joseph accurately interpreted them, and Pharaoh promoted him to become the Prime Minister of Egypt.

So Joseph was finally released from the prison and put into Pharaoh's palace after many years of unjust punishment for things he had never done. Joseph was a human being, just like you and me, and he endured harsh, unfair treatment at the hands of his own brothers and other strangers. But he continued to bear the fruit of the Spirit in abundance and forgave everyone concerned. So can you. God will always help you to forgive others if you are struggling to do so. Just ask Him for His help (James 4:2).

## Do Not Seek Revenge

Joseph would have been justified to send his brothers away empty-handed when they requested his assistance to provide food for them in the time of the severe famine and hardship that followed his promotion. But Joseph refused to be consumed with hatred and bitterness. He continued to walk in love, ensuring that his entire family had adequate provision including their little ones. Even after his father's death, he set a godly example by refusing to seek revenge, saying, "'Do not be afraid, for *am* I in the place of God? But as for you, you meant evil against me; *but* God meant it for good, in order to bring it about as *it is* this day, to save many people alive. Now therefore, do not be afraid; I will provide for you and your little ones.' And he comforted them and spoke kindly to them" (Genesis 50:19-21 NKJV).

So receive strength and comfort from Joseph's godly example by developing godly character. If you are tempted to avenge yourself, please refrain from doing so. You may feel that you are justified to seek vengeance because your loved one was brutally murdered and snatched away from you prematurely without any warning. You're hurting, and your pain is so raw to the point where it's almost unbearable.

In addition to the pain of loss, you feel like the justice system has failed you. Even though you went to court and tried to get justice done legally, unfortunately the murderer was not convicted of the crime. Both you and he know that he is guilty, but he is still a free man, a danger to society. He shows no remorse, and he is still in a position to repeat the same crime again.

Granting all of those circumstances, the Holy Bible still tells us in Romans 12:19-21 (NKJV), "Beloved, do not avenge yourselves, but *rather* give place to wrath; for it is written, *'Vengeance is Mine, I will repay,'* says the Lord. Therefore *'If your enemy is hungry, feed him; If he is thirsty, give him a drink; For in so doing you will heap coals of fire on his head.'* Do not be overcome by evil, but overcome evil with good."

So I urge you again, please don't take matters into your own hands and murder the criminal. Do not even consider hiring someone else to commit that murder on your behalf. You will regret it in the future if you do. Remember that God, who always knows best, has commanded us to be swift to hear and slow to anger and to refrain from sinning when we're angry (James 1:19-20 and Ephesians 4:26).

You are so much better than that impulse to revenge, which will only ruin your life. And besides, your deceased loved one would **definitely** never have wanted you to commit such an atrocious crime. Remember that two wrongs don't make things right; they are only two evils. We will only overcome evil with good (Romans 12:21).

And if I still haven't convinced you not to commit this horrendous crime, please consider how much you would disgrace and hurt your family members and loved ones, especially if you have young children and elderly family members who depend on you to take care of them. I urge you to consider how revenge would also affect the victim's family members, who maybe completely innocent of any wrong doing also. Therefore, we must only do unto others what we would like them to do to us (Matthew 7:12).

So obey God; refuse to sin by getting blood on your hands. Our enemy Satan will be the only one who wins if you turn to vengeance. In addition to destroying your life, you will also destroy many other lives.

So be the better person, like Jesus, Stephen, Joseph, and David were, and forgive immediately. After David had killed Goliath and the women danced and said "Saul has slain his thousands, And David his ten thousands" (1 Samuel 18:7 NKJV), Saul became jealous of David and attempted to kill him on numerous occasions. David could have avenged himself and murdered Saul. But David refused to do so. Like him, neither should you harm anyone (see Psalm 105:15; 1 Samuel 24, paying particular attention to verses 6-7). Regardless of how you feel, you do not have the right to murder anyone (Exodus 20:13).

However, during your sad circumstances, please be comforted by remembering that this situation is only temporary. "Weeping may endure for a night, but joy comes in the morning" (Psalm 30:5). Providing your loved one was born again and you are, you will see him or her in heaven one day. So the one you lost is definitely in a better place with the Lord where there is no pain, tears, or sorrow (Revelation 21:3-4).

Even if you think your loved one has died in transgression and gone to hell, you cannot be sure as to whether they had given their heart to the Lord just before slipping into eternity. All things are possible with God (Matthew 19:26). So cheer up; you may experience a pleasant surprise.

# Don't Neglect Church Attendance

You may be thinking: *How dare she mention that I should attend church when I'm feeling like this? How can anyone be so insensitive? Doesn't she have any feelings at all? I'm in shock, and I'm mourning. The last place I feel like going is to church. I want to be left alone. I don't want to see anyone. I just want to close my curtains, go to bed, curl up, and die. This excruciating pain is just too much for me.*

Dearly beloved, you can rest assured that I understand how you are feeling. Remember, I have also experienced the loss of many deeply loved and cherished ones. But what you are saying is not exactly true, as God our loving Father will never allow you or anyone else to go through anything without giving us the ability to overcome it victoriously. We may not see the victory now or even understand why we are suffering, but one day we definitely will. So your pain is not too much for you to bear. You are much stronger than you think (1 Corinthians 10:13, 13:9-12; 2 Corinthians 2:14; and Isaiah 40:28-31).

But you have to refocus your thinking. You must focus on God and the others who are left behind and who desperately need you for their survival also. Thinking dark, ugly thoughts will only lead to depression and make an already bad situation exceedingly worse. Therefore, refuse self-centeredness and self-pity. Fix your eyes on God, who is the source of all good and all of our help (see Psalm 121, paying particular attention to verses 1-2). God will certainly keep us in perfect peace when we have our minds continually stayed on Him (Isaiah 26:3).

Take comfort from the knowledge that God loves us unconditionally and eternally. Dwell on the fact that nothing shall separate us from the love of God (Romans 8:35-39).

If Jesus did everything based on His feelings, He would never have died for us on the cross at Calvary and interceded on our behalf. Despite His pain, he pled for us just before His cruel crucifixion (Luke 22:42, 23:32-34).

Seeing that God knows what's best for us, we must submit to His will. He has instructed us not to forsake the assembling of the saints. So we must continue to attend church regularly, even if we only do so to honour, love, and reverence Him (Hebrews 10:25).

## Suicide Is Never the Answer

You may be sitting in the dark somewhere contemplating suicide with a gun to your head or with a bottle of pills and alcohol. **Stop right now** where you are, and **don't kill yourself**.

Some of you may be thinking: *I'm so depressed. I've had enough. I wish it was me who had died, not my relative. My relative was a lovelier and much nicer person than I am. I'm so unworthy. I don't deserve to live, and even if I die now, nobody will ever miss me. My life has no meaning. I have nothing left to live for; so I might as well end it now. Besides, no one needs or loves me. I don't add any value to anyone else's life. All I do is take from everyone. I never add beauty or joy to anyone's life. I feel like going to bed and never waking up again. So what is the point of me going on?*

Please don't commit suicide or even consider it for one more moment. I'm beseeching you not to give place to those thoughts; you will **definitely** regret it if you do.

In the name of Jesus, I command you to wipe those dark thoughts completely out of your mind now. Renew your mind with the Word of God, and stop blaming yourself. This tragedy is not your fault. Stop listening to the lies of the devil. He is a liar, schemer, deceiver, robber, and a thief, and everything he says is false (John 8:44; Romans 8:1, 12:1; 2 Corinthians 10:3-5; Philippians 4:8; and Exodus 20:13).

I promise you that things will get better, despite how you feel now. Emotions will always come and go. So take charge of your emotions, and don't let them lead you into folly.

Dearly beloved, suicide is never the answer. You are special, loved, needed, and so very wanted. The world would suffer a great loss and injustice if you died now, and so would all of your family members and your loved ones.

Could you imagine the devastation, pain, and suffering you would cause them in addition to the heartache they are already suffering? Some of them may receive the burden of condemnation from the devil and falsely blame themselves for your suicide and untimely death. They may never be truly happy again. Is that what you want?

Please remember that you are not your own. You were purchased with the precious blood of Jesus Christ, and you belong to God (1 Corinthians 6:19-20). Besides, you are an extremely kind and loving person, certainly never selfish.

Even if I still haven't convinced you to change your mind yet, please think about your children and all of those people who really love and care about you. Put yourself in their shoes. How would you feel if they left you in that way? Can you imagine the unnecessary pain and devastation you would leave behind and all of the unanswered questions they would have if you committed this horrible, barbaric act?

Right now, I will just take the time to pray for you: *Spirit of suicide and premature death, I take authority over you in the name of Jesus. I bind you, Satan, and command you to loose every suicidal person and let them go now. I decree and declare that they will live and not die and declare the works of the Lord. God, please satisfy them and show them your salvation. Let the joy of the Lord be their strength. Let the peace of God which surpasses all understanding be theirs now and forevermore in Jesus' name, amen* (Psalm 91:15-16, 118:17; and Philippians 4:7).

If you're still contemplating suicide, there will always be horrible consequences for your actions. You won't be able to change your mind. There will always be life after death, because even though our bodies die, our spirit never does. Everyone will have to give an account to God about our lives (Luke 16:19-31 and 2 Corinthians 5:10).

## Married Couples

I'm addressing married couples now. Don't withhold sex from your spouse for unduly long periods of time after mourning, as this distance can open a door for the devil to destroy your marriage. You may be feeling disgusted and enraged at me and thinking: *How dare she mention sex to me at a time like this when I'm hurting? I'm grieving, and I don't even know if I can make it through another day. How can someone be so callous and cold hearted?*

As I previously mentioned in chapter 2, after King David and Bathsheba's first son had died because of his sin, David comforted his wife and had sexual intercourse with her. She conceived and bore him a son, whose name was Solomon, and God loved him. If King David had not reunited with his wife during their grief, they may have never had their beloved son, who became the richest king and wisest man that ever lived (2 Samuel 12:24; 1 Kings 4:30; and 2 Chronicles 9:22).

Listen to me, dearly beloved. Please do not tear up this book or flush it down the toilet in haste and anger. I cannot overemphasise how much God loves you. You are very important to Him and to so many others, probably much more than you will ever know.

Jesus paid an awfully high price for your redemption on the cross at Calvary, and, cherished one, God definitely has a wonderful plan for your life. Even though you may not see it now, I can assure you that it's really good (Jeremiah 29:11 and Ephesians 2:10). Things will get better. God is for you, not against you. He's definitely on your side (Romans 8:31).

Believe me: I'm speaking to you out of a heart of pure love and wisdom. I'm just taking dictation from the Holy Ghost, who is our helper. I'm trying to save your marriage in the long term.

I'm sure you don't want to experience the loss of your spouse in addition to the loss of your loved one. So be wise and invest in your marriage, which is very valuable, by submitting to your spouse, especially if your partner is requesting **due** conjugal rights (1 Corinthians 7:1-5). You may also be able to receive comfort from each other this way.

But if you're still not ready, you can at least cuddle and comfort each other. Gently ask your spouse to be patient and understanding. When the time is right, God will make this oneness happen for you, because patience is a fruit of the Spirit (Galatians 5:22).

# CHAPTER 5: RECEIVING HELP FROM THE CHURCH

Sadly, many people will only turn to the church for assistance when they are desperately in need of help, usually after they have exhausted every other avenue. But this should not be so (Matthew 6:33). Because God is love and He is exceedingly kind and because the church is Jesus' body (ambassadors here on this earth), I believe that every church should prepare in advance to comfort those who grieve. Where possible, churches should establish a bereavement fund and also a miscellaneous fund which they make available to help people in a time of need, especially as some people will only listen to the preaching of the gospel after they have experienced acts of kindness directly from the church.

Because this book mainly deals with helping people overcome grief, I would strongly suggest that if your church does not have a bereavement fund, you should seriously consider having one. Speak to your leaders about creating one so that especially needy, vulnerable, grieving people like widows, orphans, single parents, students, and people who are unemployed, disabled, homeless, or elderly can benefit from it in a time of need.

Depending upon how big the congregation of the church is, you can create a department which deals with helping bereaved and hurting people through counselling, if one does not already exist. I strongly recommend that everyone in this department should be faithful, strong, committed, born-again Christians, preferably Holy Spirit-filled believers who are loving, patient, tender-hearted, kind, and compassionate. The department should create a team that consists of counsellors, prayer intercessors, and people who are willing to help others (Acts 6:1-3; 1 Corinthians 13:4; and Colossians 3:23-24).

However, I don't believe that the church should insist that every candidate should have to have a degree in counselling in order to do Christian counselling in the church. This requirement could discriminate against godly people who are anointed and called by God to counsel hurting people. With a little training from the church, those without degrees could turn out to be excellent counsellors. A requirement for degrees could also result in choosing qualified un-called people who are void of the fruit of the Spirit and compassion. So with much prayer, supplication, and God's direction, both qualified and unqualified people should be considered for these positions.

A few years ago, the Lord instructed me to create a bereavement fund in a church that I attended. With my former pastor's permission, I raised funds in church for this fund by selling some of the books I had written in addition to some other Christian CD and DVD teaching materials I'd produced and giving a portion of the proceeds of the sales to the church, in addition to doing another fundraising activity.

Of course, before proceeding to doing anything, you should always pray and ask for God's assistance with your new endeavour. By inviting God's help and guidance, you will be acknowledging Him in all of your ways and opening the door for His much needed wisdom, provision, instruction, and direction (Proverbs 3:5-6 and Philippians 4:19). But if your church does not have a department entitled the Ministry of Helps or something similar, you should seriously consider setting up one with several willing volunteers, with the permission of your pastor or the person in charge.

This department should have a meeting and a leader, and a deputy leader should be selected. The leader should proceed by discussing how often to have fundraising activities, for example, once a month or once per quarter or whatever is convenient for everyone involved.

After this meeting has occurred, a venue should also be selected for where the fundraising activities should take place. A rota should be implemented. However, in order to ensure it runs smoothly, every team member should be in agreement with the days and times they are allocated to do fundraising (Psalm 133).

Procedures should also be implemented as to how to report absences of members who are unable to attend because of unforeseen circumstances such as emergencies or family crises. Volunteers should stand by to replace the absentees whenever necessary.

# Opening a Bank Account for the Bereavement Fund

If your church does not already have a bank account specifically for this purpose, I would encourage you to open an account entitled Bereavement Fund, with the permission of your pastor or whoever is in charge of course. And all of the money raised and donated to this fund and all future donations should be placed directly into this bank account, unless funds are immediately allocated and distributed to the bereaved as soon as they are raised.

# Fundraising Activities for the Bereavement Fund

*Fundraising Activity 1*

Here are a few examples of how churches can raise money for the bereavement fund. The church can sell many items, including pens, pencils, books, toys, costume jewellery, clothes, and non-perishable food items like canned and bottled foods in addition to having cake sales and church fairs.

In addition to these sales, purchasing or hiring a bouncy castle and charging children a small sum of money for about a five-minute session of bouncing may be a good idea for raising funds. A bouncy castle may be a profitable activity, especially if a church has a large Sunday school.

Like any other investment, the castle may take a little while to become profitable, especially if you have just purchased it. But it should become profitable in the foreseeable future, depending on how often you use it. An even better idea is to ask someone or several willing members of the church to donate a bouncy castle for this purpose, as the donation would minimise cost and ensure immediate profit from this activity.

However, the children should be carefully supervised by a responsible adult or adults, depending upon the number of children partaking in the activity. Please ensure that you follow the manufacturer's and government's safety guidelines when using the bouncy castle. For example, children should not be allowed to possess sharp objects or things that can puncture the bouncy castle when they are playing, neither should they wear high-heeled shoes when bouncing. In fact, they should not be wearing any shoes at all when playing on the bouncy castle.

Please ensure that the bouncy castle is not overcrowded in order to prevent unnecessary accidents and ensure that the bouncy castle is not damaged or completely destroyed due to abuse. Also ensure that only children of the correct height and weight only are allowed to play on the bouncy castle. Enlist first aiders to be available on site to assist if any accidents occur during play.

Care should also be taken in transporting and storing this valuable piece of equipment in order to ensure its longevity. For example, it should not be stored in an excessively hot area or too close to heaters.

This fun activity can also be a great tool of assistance to encourage evangelism in your church and Sunday school. The team leader can advertise this event over a period of time, perhaps a month or two in advance, and encourage everyone else to invite friends who have young children or know un-churched people who have young children.

The Sunday school children should be encouraged to do the same, and if required, parents or other volunteers from the church can offer the visiting children lifts to church, of course with the permission of their parents or guardians. The children's' parents or other responsible adults can also be invited and encouraged to attend.

## *Fund Raising Activity 2*

While this activity is taking place, another group of church volunteers can offer to paint children's faces for a small sum of money. Before proceeding to do so, please ensure that you have written permission from the parents or responsible guardians of the children if their parents or guardians are absent. Also ensure that the children are not allergic to any of the paints.

And in order to avoid strife and children being disappointed, the team should have samples of the face paintings they intend to paint on the children's faces clearly displayed for everyone to see. This precaution will ensure that both parents and children will know what images are available. If parents dislike the images, their children will not be allowed to have their faces painted.

If you make these preparations, volunteers or children will not be scolded by angry parents. Children will not be forced to wash off their paintings immediately, which may result in tears. You will not see children being taken home immediately, never allowed to return to what supposed have been an innocent, fun activity.

Care should also be taken when selecting the images so that no scary images are used in this activity, as scary pictures can negatively affect children, even causing some of them to have nightmares or wet their beds.

*Fund Raising Activity 3*

In addition to this activity, the church can also raise funds by selling refreshments. Leaders can ask church members to donate suitable refreshments for sale and allocate the sales profit to the bereavement fund. However, you may need to contact your local council to ensure that the correct procedures are in place for you to serve food on the premises. You may need a licence and a food hygiene certificate before proceeding.

## *Fund Raising Activity 4*

Your pastor or leader could increase the bereavement fund by encouraging church members to contribute voluntarily to the bereavement fund from time to time or whenever the Holy Spirit prompts them to do so. Members should not be pressured into giving. However, they can be gently encouraged to give from a pure, willing heart and not grudgingly or out of necessity, for God loves a cheerful or hilarious giver. Remember that everyone who lends to the poor lends to God (2 Corinthians 9:6-7 and Proverbs 19:17).

## A Word of Caution

Even though many people, including Christians, do fundraising by having raffles and bingo, I don't recommend this strategy because those activities are a form of gambling. Gambling is sinful and can lead to addictions later on in life (Proverbs 13:11).

# Additional Help for the Hurting

*Establish a Visiting Department in the Church*

Your church can also set up a visiting department consisting of several willing, committed, and reliable Christian volunteers and counsellors who will visit church members and people in the local community who are in need of care and help.

You can follow the principles previously mentioned in this book about how to set up a department for the bereavement fund. Members from this new department can set up a rota system which would allow every member when required to visit bereaved families, especially the recently bereaved. Be sure to make a note of the anniversaries of all the bereaved families in the church, and remember to visit, help, and encourage them around that painful time of the year especially.

Members from this department can also help the bereaved families with making the funeral arrangements if they require help, as the time of loss can be very painful and stressful for families. A member of the department should also be in charge of allocating financial support for these families for the purchasing of wreaths, tombstones, et cetera. Or volunteers can accompany the bereaved families and financially assist them while they are purchasing these items.

However, in order to ensure accountability and prevent strife or the misspending of funds, every member of the department should be in agreement, especially if large amounts of money are being withdrawn and allocated to families.

Members from the visiting department can also telephone and visit people who are absent from church, especially when they are hospitalised or at home and too sick to attend church. In addition to phone calls, some members can also host church services in the homes of sick people if required, especially if the person is house-bound for a long period of time. The church services don't have to be lengthy, but they can still consist of prayer, praise, worship, and Bible study.

Providing a kind of mobile church will help vulnerable, bereaved, sick, and hurting people not to feel neglected or isolated. Instead, they can confidently know that they are loved by God and the church family. They will also be spiritually fed, more emotionally stable, and less likely to become suicidal. Willing volunteers from this department can also assist those in need of help, especially the bereaved, house-bound, sick, and elderly, to do chores like gardening, cleaning, shopping, and cooking.

Because you are reading this book, I believe that either you desire to help someone who is bereaved or you're bereaved and in need of help. Therefore, please feel free to contact a good Christian church or ministry, explain your situation to them, and ask for their assistance. Don't ever be too proud to ask, because everyone needs help from time to time. I'm sure the church will assist you, or if they are not financially strong enough to do so, they will at least pray for you and point you in the right direction.

I pray that God will use this book as a tool to comfort you and many others in their time of need, give you peace, beauty for ashes, the oil of joy for mourning, and the garment of praise for a heavy spirit. I also pray that you will know the length, depth, and height of God's love and that everyone who is not saved will be born-again (Isaiah 61:1-3; 2 Corinthians 1:3-5; Ephesians 3:17-18; 1 Timothy 2:4; and 2 Peter 3:9). I pray for you in Jesus' name, amen.

## A Prayer for Salvation

If you are not born-again and if you desire to make Jesus Christ the Lord of your life, please say this prayer aloud immediately.

"Father, I know that I have sinned and fallen short of Your glory. I believe that Your Son Jesus died on the cross at Calvary to save me from all my sins. I confess with my mouth that Jesus is my Lord and Saviour, and I believe in my heart that God raised Him from the dead. I'm now a new creation in Christ. I'm a born-again Christian. Please fill me with your Holy Spirit with the evidence of speaking in new tongues. Thanks for hearing and answering my prayer. In Jesus' name, amen."

Now open your mouth, yield to the Holy Spirit, and speak with new tongues in your heavenly prayer language. Congratulations! Welcome to the family of God. You have made the best decision of your life. You are now a born-again Christian, and the Holy Spirit is living inside you (Romans 3:23, 10:9-10; 2 Corinthians 5:17; Acts 2:1-20; 1 Corinthians 14:2; Mark 16:17; and 1 John 5:14-15).

If you spoke in new tongues, you are filled with the Holy Spirit. Even if you didn't, don't worry about it. You are still born again and can receive the baptism of the Holy Spirit another time.

I didn't receive the baptism of the Holy Spirit immediately when I was born again, and neither did many others. I received the baptism of the Holy Spirit about five years or so afterwards, when I received teachings about the Holy Spirit. Mature Christians laid hands on me and prayed for me, and then I began to speak in new tongues. So don't be dismayed. And don't hesitate to contact our ministry if you require prayer to receive the baptism of the Holy Spirit, as we will be honoured to pray with you.

However, I do encourage everyone who has received a heavenly prayer language to pray in tongues daily in addition to praying in your native language. As you do so, you will build yourself spiritually, quicken your Christian maturity and understanding of the Bible, keep yourself in love with God, and develop your prayer life (1 Corinthians 14:2, 4 and Jude 1:20-21).

I also recommend that you purchase a copy of my book ***Triumphant in the Lord (revised edition),*** which will be released shortly. Please do **not** purchase any **new copies of the original book *Triumphant in the Lord*** because this book should be out of print. I terminated my contract with the publishers several years ago, and I do not receive any royalties for the sale of those books. Any new copies of these books are illegally printed.

Therefore, whether you have spoken in tongues or not, reading **_Triumphant in the Lord (revised edition)_** will help you understand more about your heavenly prayer language and the baptism of the Holy Spirit, along with many other wonderful, biblical truths. You can also purchase other teaching materials about the baptism of the Holy Spirit directly from our website.

Please join a good Christian church that teaches the Bible and is led by the Holy Spirit, and partner with godly ministries as the Holy Spirit leads you. This involvement will accelerate your spiritual growth. Also, please contact our ministry and let us know what God has done for you through reading this book.

I pray that the God of comfort will continue to comfort and strengthen you and your loved ones, that He will turn around for your good everything that Satan meant for your harm, and that you will enjoy a fruitful and prosperous life, in Jesus' name, amen (Genesis 50:20; 2 Corinthians 1:3-5; and 3 John 2). Continue to live for God, resting assured that He has an abundance of good things in store for you (Jeremiah 29:11).

# ABOUT THE AUTHOR

Pamela D. Daniels is the pastor and founder of Fishers of Men Pamela Daniels Ministries and Faith Builders Church United Kingdom, which is a part of the Ministry. She is also a Christian songwriter.

She has been in full-time ministry preaching and teaching the gospel of Jesus Christ for over sixteen years. She is committed to taking the gospel to a lost and hurting world. She wrote her first book *Triumphant in the Lord* in 2009, her second book *228 Days of Wisdom* in 2013, her third book *God Is Willing To Make You Whole* in 2014, and her fourth book *51 Keys to Effective Prayer* in 2015. She endeavours to go into the world and preach the gospel and expects God to confirm His Word with signs and wonders following the preached Word. She also plans to have a worldwide television broadcast.

Learn more about Fishers of Men Pamela Daniels Ministries

(Faith Builders Church United Kingdom)

By visiting our website at **www.fompdm.org**

# Books by Reverend Pamela D. Daniels

*Triumphant in the Lord*

*Triumphant in the Lord (revised edition)*

*228 Days of Wisdom*

*God Is Willing To Make You Whole*

*51 Keys to Effective Prayer*

*Receiving Comfort from God and Overcoming Grief*